FRANKLIN WATTS
LONDON•SYDNEY

Franklin Watts

First published in Great Britain in 2016 by
The Watts Publishing Group

Text © Lynne Benton 2016
Illustrations © Roger Simó 2016

Series Editor: Jackie Hamley
Series Advisor: Catherine Glavina
Series Designer: Peter Scoulding

A CIP catalogue record for this book is available
from the British Library.

ISBN 978 1 4451 4569 3 (hbk)
ISBN 978 1 4451 4586 0 (pbk)
ISBN 978 1 4451 4591 4 (library ebook)

Printed in China

FSC
www.fsc.org
MIX
Paper from
responsible sources
FSC® C104740

Franklin Watts
An imprint of
Hachette Children's Group
Part of The Watts Publishing Group
Carmelite House
50 Victoria Embankment
London EC4Y 0DZ

An Hachette UK company.
www.hachette.co.uk

www.franklinwatts.co.uk

Archie was a bat.

Archie's family lived in a big tree. Every day they slept in the branches.

Every night they flew out to catch insects.

But Archie didn't catch insects. He did flying tricks instead.

He swooped,

he scooped

and he looped the loop.

No, Archie, bats don't do tricks," said Mum.

"But it's fun," said Archie.

One night, Grandpa said, "The council are going to chop down our tree!"

"Oh no!" said the bats.

Archie worried too, but he flew off and did his tricks as usual.

12

"That bat is looping the loop. It's amazing!" said a man.

Archie saw a poster.

He had an idea.

He told all his friends about his idea.

Archie showed them how
to do his tricks.

"Tomorrow we'll show everyone," he said.

Next night the bats swooped and looped around in the sky.

A crowd gathered to watch them.

"Wow! They are so clever!" everyone said.

Next night a bigger
crowd gathered.

Archie and his team did their tricks again.

Amazing!

25

The next night, even more people were there.

They all carried
newspapers that said:
"The Amazing Acrobats!"

Grandpa beamed. "Because of Archie, the council have decided not to chop down our tree," he said.

Puzzle 1

Put these pictures in the correct order.
Now tell the story in your own words.
Can you think of a different ending?

excited   scared

thrilled

worried   nervous

delighted

Choose the words which best describe Archie and which best describe Grandpa in the pictures. Can you think of any more?

Answers

Puzzle 1

The correct order is:

1e, 2c, 3a, 4f, 5b, 6d

Puzzle 2

Archie   The correct words are excited, thrilled.
The incorrect word is scared.

Grandpa   The correct words are nervous, worried.
The incorrect word is delighted.

Look out for more stories:

For details of all our titles go to: www.franklinwatts.co.uk